LITTLE BOOK OF

Knitting

With **Clare Davies**

at The Gilliangladrag Fluff-a-torium

LITTLE BOOK OF
Knitting

First published in the UK in 2014

© Demand Media Limited 2014

www.demand-media.co.uk

Printed and bound in Europe

ISBN 978-1-910270-81-3

Contents

Introduction

Learn to knit with me Clare Davies - knitting teacher at The Gilliangladrag Fluff-a-torium. I like to think I'm a patient knitting and crochet teacher and I regularly hold classes in the studio. Over the coming pages, I will share with you the basics to get you started, and then move you on to some simple projects to practice what you've learnt.

You'll be knitting in no time!

Chapter 1

The Basics
Things you'll need for knitting...

Yarns comes in lots of different thicknesses and weights. Chunky yarns knit up faster and are warmer, whereas finer yarns can be used for delicate work but take longer to knit.

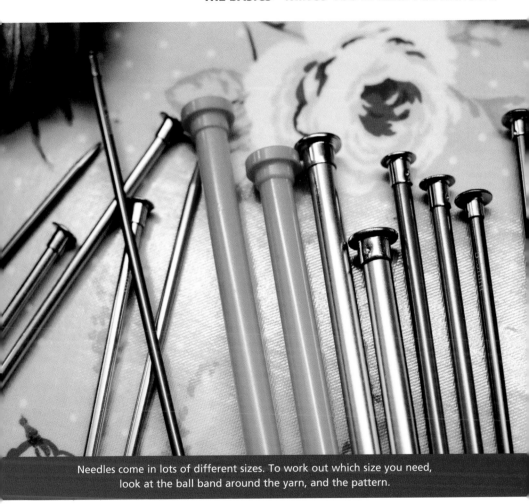

Needles come in lots of different sizes. To work out which size you need, look at the ball band around the yarn, and the pattern.

There are lots of things that are useful to have around when knitting, such as a tape measure, bodkin (large eyed blunt needle) stitch markers, row counter and scissors etc.

Chapter 2

Getting Started

How to cast on...

1. Make a slip knot by looping the yarn and pushing the long end through the loop.

2. Push the needle into the loop you've pushed through; hold both tails; one tail will pull the knot tight, and the other tail will pull the knot up to the needle.

3. With the stitch on the Left hand needle, push the right needle underneath the stitch and towards the back of the left. Hold these two needles with the left hand thumb and forefinger.

4. Lift the yarn with your right hand, and bring it anticlockwise around the back of the right hand needle and through the middle of the two.

5. With the tip of the RH needle, pull the yarn through the loop.

6. Pull a large loop, then hook it onto the LH needle by bringing the needle towards you and under the loop. You have cast on one stitch, two in total.

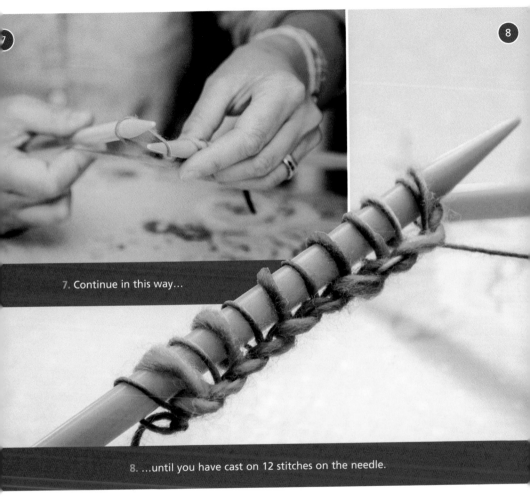

7. Continue in this way...

8. ...until you have cast on 12 stitches on the needle.

Chapter 3

How to Knit a Scarf

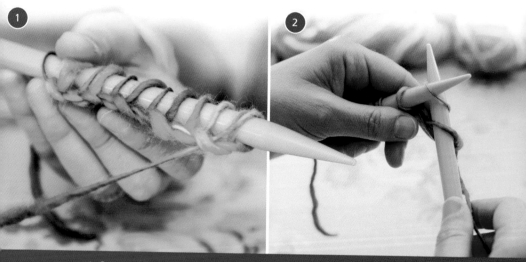

1. Cast on 12 stitches. 2. Hold the needle with the stitches in the left hand. Push the tip of the RH needle under the 1st stitch and hold at back.

3. Lift the yarn with your right hand, pass it anti clockwise round the back of the needles and through the middle of the two.

4. With the tip of RH needle pull the yarn under the bar of the stitch.

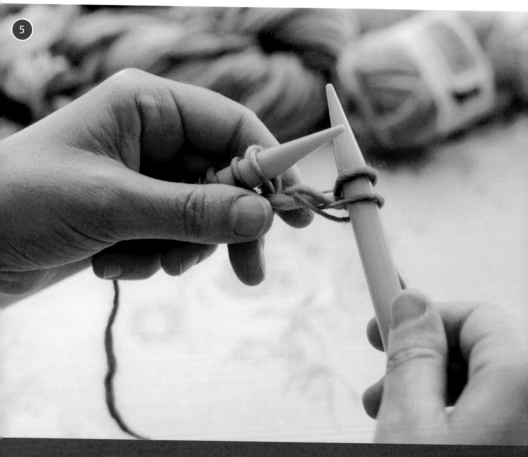

5. That stitch has been knitted, so push the old stitch off the LH needle.

6

6. Continue to knit each stitch until all the stitches on the LH needle have been knitted onto the RH needle. Swap the needle with the stitches into the LH and knit the next row, repeat until scarf is the length you desire. This is called **garter stitch**, when you knit every row. And now to cast off...

How to cast off & tassels...

1. Knit 2 stitches on to RH needle.

2. Use the LH needle to pull the 1st stitch knitted up and over the end of the RH needle.

3. Knit another stitch onto RH needle and repeat until only 1 stitch is remaining.

4. Pull stitch larger, cut a 10cm tail, and push the end of the tail through the loop to secure.

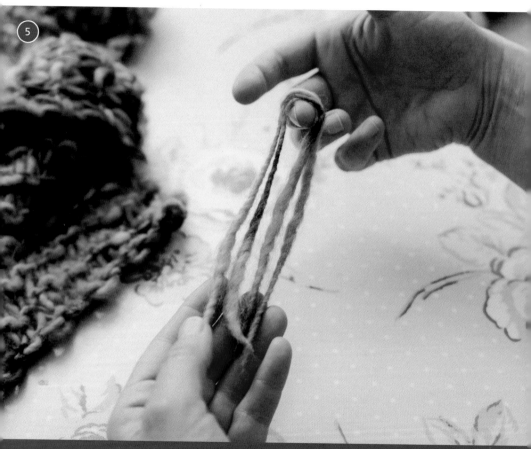

5. Keep 10m of yarn to make the tassels before you start the scarf. Decide how long you want the tassels and cut the yarn into pieces twice as long as this.

6. Decide how you will space the tassels evenly. Take 2 of the pieces and fold the cut yarn lengths in half. Pass these folded loops through an end stitch of your scarf.

7. Pass the tails through the loop...

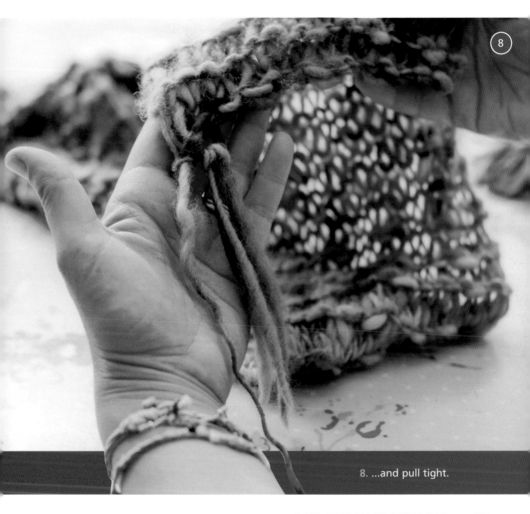

8. ...and pull tight.

Chapter 4.

Different Knitting Stitches

Purl Stitch & Stocking Stitch...

1. Insert the RH needle underneath and towards the front of the stitch – coming out towards you.

2. Wrap the yarn anticlockwise around the right hand needle, through the middle of the needles, and towards the front.

3. Pull the yarn through the stitch towards the back.

4. Push the old stitch with the left hand off the needle.

Stocking stitch is when you knit a row and then purl the next, alternating like this all the way through. To know whether to knit or purl, hold the stitches in the left hand, ready to work. If the bobbles are facing you, it is a purl row. If the flat 'v's are facing you, knit the next row.

Moss Stitch...

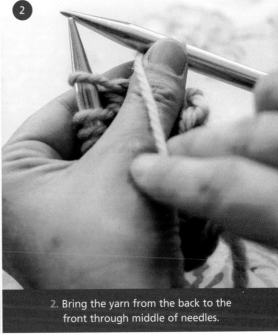

1. Knit one stitch.

2. Bring the yarn from the back to the front through middle of needles.

3. Purl the next stitch.

4. Bring the Yarn from the front to the back through the middle of the needles to knit the next stitch, and so on. The next row, knit the purl stitches and purl the knit stitches throughout.

This is what your finished moss stitch will look like.

Double Moss Stitch...

1. The first row of double moss stitch is the same as the first row of single moss stitch; K1P1 all the way across.

2. Row 2: instead of alternating (like single moss stitch) knit the knit stitches and purl the purl stitches. The knit stitches can be recognised by their flat 'v' and the purls look like bobbles – or 'pearls'.

3. Repeat this two row pattern for the length required.

Pattern Stitch...

Now you can knit and purl, you can use them in different ways to create patterns and textures.

Changing Yarn Colour...

Top Tip:
"Try and change colour on a "knit row" if you can."

1

1. Take the new yarn and tie a knot around the old yarn.

2. Pull tight and slide the knot of the new colour yarn up to the needle.

3. Start working with the new colour.

If you follow these instructions you will end up with a clean line where the colour changes.

Counting Rows & Stitches...

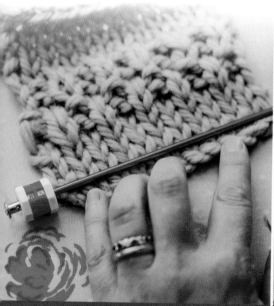

Count the rows of your knitting by counting the little "v" shapes, - each "v" is one row. You can use a row counter, just turn move it on each row that you finish.

To count the stitches across the row, each little "v" is one stitch.

Sewing Up...

1. You've finished knitting! Now you need to sew it all together. There are many ways to do this – this way is using oversewing. Thread a bodkin or wool needle with your yarn. Put the wrong sides together & secure the yarn at the beginning of the seam.

2. Sew from the back to the front over and over to the end, taking care to sew evenly.

3. Try to avoid the cast on and cast off edges, for a neat finish.

4. Sew in the end of the yarn neatly too.

5. Repeat with the other square to form a patchwork.

Chapter 5

Learning to Increase and Decrease

Increasing...

1. Cast on 2 stitches.

2. Insert needle knit wise and pull stitch through, without pushing it off the left needle.

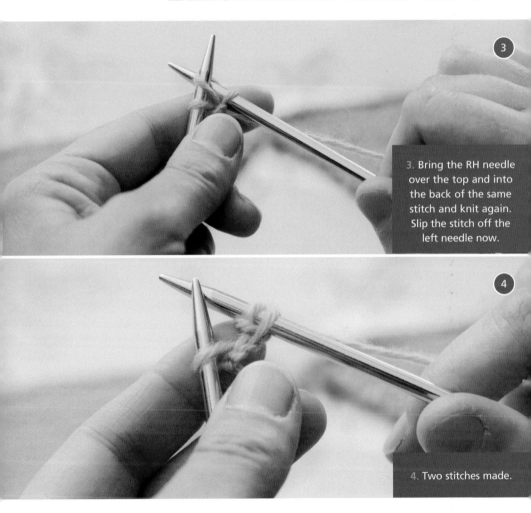

3. Bring the RH needle over the top and into the back of the same stitch and knit again. Slip the stitch off the left needle now.

4. Two stitches made.

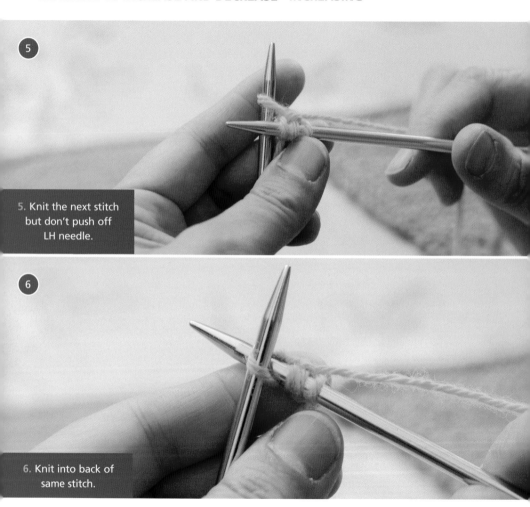

5

5. Knit the next stitch but don't push off LH needle.

6

6. Knit into back of same stitch.

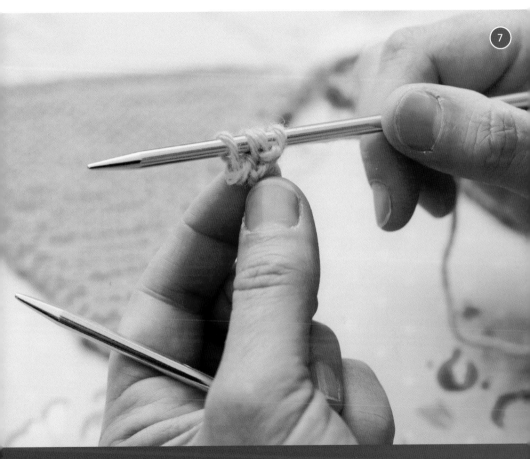

7. 4 stitches made. Use this increase when a pattern "inc" (also known as kfb or knit forward and back).

8. To knit the rest of the triangle or pennant, now knit 2 more rows, increasing at each end of the 3rd row, but knit the 1st stitch of the increase row, then increase one, knit to the last two stitches of the same row, increase in the 1st stitch and knit the last stitch. Increasing one stitch in on each side, will keep the edges crisp.

Decreasing...

1. You can also make the flags by decreasing. Cast on 30 stitches and knit one row. Next row knit one stitch and knit the next two stitches together, knit to the last 3 stitches.

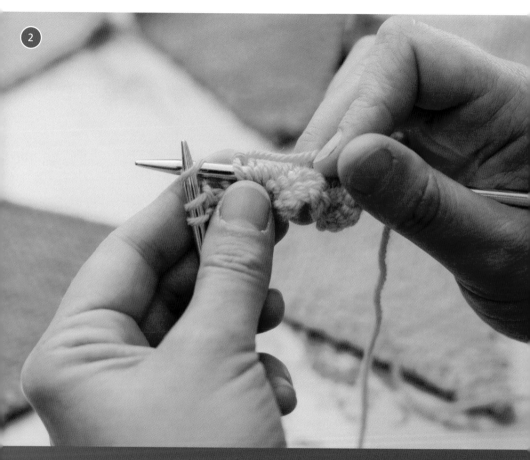

2. Insert RH needle into next stitch and slip across on to RH needle without knitting.

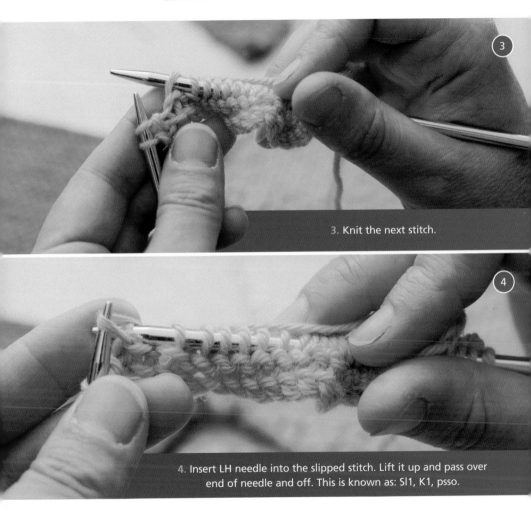

3

3. Knit the next stitch.

4

4. Insert LH needle into the slipped stitch. Lift it up and pass over end of needle and off. This is known as: Sl1, K1, psso.

5. Decrease in the same way at each end of every 3rd row, until 4 stitches remain, K2tog twice, then knit the last two together and fasten off.

6. Use a matching yarn to sew the top corners of the triangles together to create your bunting. Sew the ends in neatly.

Chapter 6

Putting what you've learnt into practise

Make a mug hug with buttonhole...

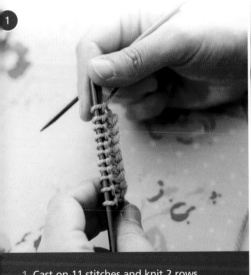

1. Cast on 11 stitches and knit 2 rows.

2. Knit 4 stitches, cast off 2 by knitting the next 2 stitches onto the RH needle.

3. Cast off one, knit another, and cast that one off too. Knit to end of row.

4. Knit 3, then Knit forward and back in the next stitch 4 times. For the 3rd stitch bring the yarn between the needles and purl. For the 4th stitch bring the yarn back through the needles and knit. Knit to end of row.

5. Knit back across all the stitches.

6. Knit another 6 or 8 rows, then increase at each end of the next 3 rows, then knit every row until the hug reaches around your mug. Cast off. Find and sew a button to fit.

Now keep your tea warm!

Making a rose and a leaf...

To make the rose:

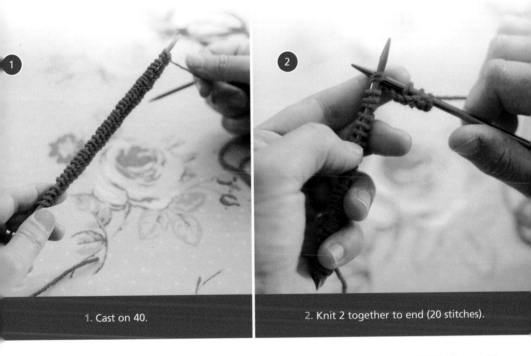

1. Cast on 40.

2. Knit 2 together to end (20 stitches).

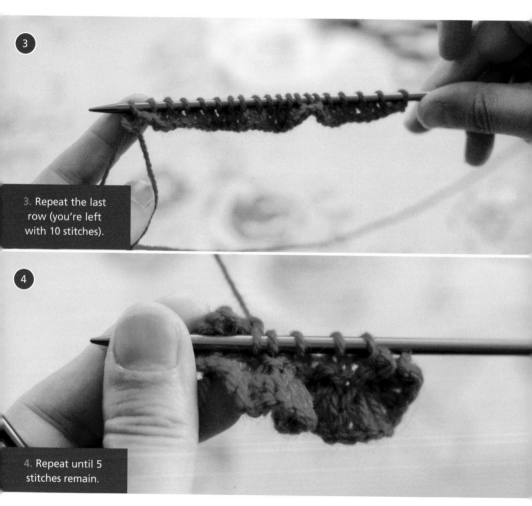

3. Repeat the last row (you're left with 10 stitches).

4. Repeat until 5 stitches remain.

5

5. Cut yarn & thread through the remaining stitches.

6

6. Use the end of the yarn to join the flower together.

7. Sew on button for centre.

8. For a larger flower, knit more rows before reducing.

1

To Make the leaf:
Use similar sized yarn and needles to the flower. CO 3 sts

Row 1: **Kfb, K1, Kfb (5 sts)**
Row 2: **K**
Row 3: **Kfb, K1, P1, K1, Kfb (7 sts)**
Row 4: **K**
Row 5: **Kfb, K2, P1, K2, Kfb (9 sts)**
Row 6: **K**
Row 7: **Kfb, K3, P1, K3, Kfb (11 sts)**
Row 8: **K**
Row 9: **K5, P1, K5**

Rows 10 to 13: repeat rows 8 and 9 twice more

Row 14: K

Row 15: K2tog, K3, P1, K3, K2tog (9 sts)

Row 16: K

Row 17: K2tog, K2, P1, K2, K2tog (7sts)

Row 18: K

Row 19: K2tog, K1, P1, K1, K2tog (5 sts)

Row 20: K

Row 21: K2tog, P1, K2tog (3sts)

Row 22: K

Row 23: Sl1, K2tog, psso and fasten off.

Chapter 8.

Finishing techniques
Blocking...

1. To create a professional finish, most knitting needs to be pressed or blocked. Take a damp cloth; pin the knitting to the ironing board in the shape desired.

2. Lay the damp cloth over the knitting and gently steam without too much pressure, avoiding ribbing and patterned stitches such as moss stitch.

Chapter 9.

Moving on...
Top Tips &
Advice for the future

Dropped Stitches...

You've noticed that you've dropped a stitch!

1. Knit up to where you've dropped the stitch. With the right side facing you, take another needle or a crochet hook and put the hook through the dropped stitch.

2. Pull the yarn through the dropped stitch.

3. Repeat...

4. ...i.e. take the hook out and put it in again through the front of the stitch and pull the yarn through again.

5. Place the stitch safely onto the left hand needle.

Picking up stitches...

Don't panic if you have to undo your knitting.

1. Take a needle in your right hand, and thread each stitch back onto it.
Pick up each stitch with the right hand side towards you if possible.

Holding the yarn - some advice...

1. With the work ready in the left hand, pull the yarn towards you....

2. ...with your right hand little finger.

3. Wrap the yarn around your little finger.

4. Hold the right hand needle like a pencil with the yarn coming between your forefinger and middle finger.

5. Use your forefinger to pick up the yarn and wrap it round to knit. The yarn will sit on your forefinger nail and your whole hand slides up to hook the yarn around. Your hands should be relaxed!

You'll have it mastered in no time!

Abbreviations...

dec	decrease(ing)
inc	increase(ing)
k	knit
kfb	knit into the front and back of the next stitch
k2tog	knit two stitches together
kwise	knitwise
m1	make one stitch, by picking up the horizontal loop before next stitch and knitting into back of it
p	purl
p2tog	purl two stitches together
psso	pass slipped stitch over
pwise	purlwise
rem	remain(ing)
rep	repeat(ing)
RS	right side
skpo	slip 1, knit 1, pass slipped stitch over

sl 1	slip one stitch
sl st	slip stitch
ssk	one by one, slip the next two stitches knitwise. Put your left needle through the front loops of both slipped stitches and knit them together.
st(s)	stitch(es)
st st	stocking stitch (RS row k, WS row p)
tbl	through the back of the loop(s)
WS	wrong side
yfwd	yarn forward (between knit sts)
yon	yarn over needle (between a purl and a knit st)
yrn	yarn round the needle (between purl sts and between a knit and a purl st)
( )	work instructions inside the brackets as many times as instructed

Design & Artwork: ALEX YOUNG

Photography: ED SCHOFIELD

Published by: DEMAND MEDIA LIMITED

Publisher: JASON FENWICK

Written by: CLARE DAVIES